DEDICATION

Many of my poems were written during the travels of my life. These are things I have seen, experienced, and felt throughout my journey. These are my feelings and how I've seen my experiences during my life's passages.

I dedicate this book to my dear mother, Alma Sayles, who gave me life and taught me the values I cherish. Thank you, Mom, for being my hero. I only wish I could be half the women you were.

To my daughter, Dawn H. Mascoll, my friend, my lawyer, and my joy. Thank you for your devoted love, your inner beauty, and being the wind beneath my wings.

And finally, I can't thank my cousin, Cookie, enough for her patience during the writing of my poems. Thank you for listening.

D1507693

ACKNOWLEDGMENTS

A special thank you to all of my colleagues at
the R.J. Bailey School. I appreciate all of your support.

To my Arubian friends, thank you for making
your home my paradise.

A special thank you to Dawn H. Mascoll, Esq,
Karen Mallory Johnson, Barbara Broadnax,
and Elizabeth Castro for your support.

And a warm and special thank you to my editor,
Leah Lakins, Founder and Chief Creative Officer
of Fresh Eyes Editorial Services, for making
my book a reality.

TABLE OF CONTENTS

TABLE OF CONTENTS

INTRODUCTION

Each page you turn

Pieces of my soul

Sharing my thoughts

Being very bold

Enjoy my words

They are from my heart

This is my story

For the most part

PART ONE

Never Forgotten

And Then There Were None

We see them come

We see them go

Along the way friendships grow

Laughter shared

Tears feared

Becoming sisters throughout the years

Secrets shared

Sadness spared

Compassion always there

Happy thoughts

Friendships never fade

Feelings

I love the way you laugh

Your eyes tell a story

They glitter and focus

On life and its glory

Friendship

Remember when we laughed and sang

Remember when that phone constantly

Rang

Remember our first big dance in town

That made us unique and renowned

Remember the disappointments

We shared as one

Some people wouldn't believe it could

Be done

Yes, we do have some warm memories

And keepsakes

That could not be shaken by

Any earthquake

We function as one, which was so seldom

Done

Yes, sit back and remember those good

Old days

And then question, "Why such a good

friendship had to fade?"

Hey Girl, What's Happening?

The phrase you always used

Laughing, singing, or taking a

Snooze

You looked, listened, and went along with

The crowd

Some things we said were not allowed

We had fun whatever we did

Club meetings, dancing or just being

A kid

Your style and your smile will truly be

Missed

We remember you saying, "Hey Girl!"

And sealed it with a kiss

Just Having Fun
1279

Skipping rope with my friends

Hoping this day doesn't end

Playing Potsie and Red Rover too

Hoping the boys choose you

Red Light, Green Light, lots of fun

Giant Steps were hard for some

Mother May I and Ring-A-Levio

Time always ran out

We had to go

Hide-N-Seek was the best

Lasting friendships withstood the test

Music Man

Your infectious smile

Smooth acting ways

Very unique one must say

That pride in your stride

Twinkle in your eye

Made you that number one guy

Words of wisdom

Giving signs of hope

Helping many to cope

Saying goodbye is hard to do

You're now a thousand miles away

Never Forgotten

Had a lot of great days

Not enough years

Often thinking of you, my friend

While holding back the tears

You shared your love

You gave your joy

Guiding me all the way

The memory of your friendship

Lingers each and every day

Piece of Mine

Still as the night, peaceful and

Serene

Blue water, the bluest you've ever

Seen

Gentle breeze puts you at ease

Hallelujah, Hallelujah, my Aruba

A little piece of heaven

Tranquility galore

Relaxing in paradise

What are you waiting for?

Together A Long Time

We go back oh so many years

Friendship so deep because we cared

High school is where it all began

Running to class before the late bell rang

Your personality captured the crowd

Walking the halls

Girl, you were so loud

Homework was not your specialty

Doing more than one was my cup of tea

Shared my worst assignment with you

So I thought

Little did I know I would be caught

The teacher was wise and passed you

Looked at me and said, " What did you do?"

That's what I get for helping my friend

For our friendship, I'd do it all over again

PART TWO

All in the Family

A Letter To An Angel

How do you write to an angel?

An angel who has guided you all
throughout your life

With love, tenderness, and lots of advice.

What do you say to an angel whose warmth,
and wisdom has

strengthened you and has prepared
you for your life's journey?

You simply thank your guardian angel for her kindness,
her strength, and devoted love.

My angel taught me to accept the things
I cannot change.

Mom, you were always there with
your angelic smile.

You are that special angel that watches
and protects me in all my

endeavors.

Thank you for you.

Love, Boojie

A Letter to Dawn

I have been blessed with a wonderful daughter

How does one define wonderful?

She's unusually good, very capable, amazing,

and phenomenal.

I say all these positive words because you're mine.

You have never given me a day of trouble.

This is remarkable.

You see, my dear daughter, I'm blessed

to have you in my life.

Thank you for being my joy and for

the great love we share.

Love, Mommie

Looking Back

Looking back over life's journey

There's so much to be thankful for

Love of family and friends

Whom I adore

As I reflect on memories

I cherish the gifts given to me

Love of family, love of friends

That special love helped shape me

To be me

Loving Things

I love a lot of things I'd never change

Cousins, friends, all the same

I love the way they comfort you

With silly talks, smiles, whatever they do

I love the depth of our strong faith

The belief in God

No matter what it takes

I love the simple joy we share

Knowing how much someone cares

I love my family and their strong ways

Makes me cherish those good old days

My Chewy

My granddog Chewy loves to play

Keeps me up night and day

Go Fetch is his favorite pastime

Trying to catch my breath is mine

Mother

You left us with a rich legacy

And still we shed the tears

Losing you is still so deep

After all those many years

I've tried so hard to understand

Just why you had to go

I guess the Almighty had his reasons

Reasons I'll never know

Time has passed, memories still deep inside

Now I understand your goodbye

Sisters

Sisters share more than parents

Love, rooms, friends, and patience

That special love that binds them close

Is not always shared by most

Secrets, girl talk, giggles, and all

Keeps that woven love strong as I'm told

Remember the love the two of you share

Thanking God you are both still here

The Fabulous Sisters

They're back in town

Laughing, singing, and messing around

These famous ladies are related you know

Get one sister angry, they'll tell you where to go

Pretty, elegant is a part of their fame

Looking fabulous is their road game

The years have gone by, life has been good

Loving, sharing all that they could

Growing older, still very close

Looking even better, much better than most

Enjoyed life's journey and all its pleasures

Their life, their closeness, is to be treasured

PART THREE

In Search of Me

Look At Me

Faces, faces, lost in a crowd

Signs of loneliness, crying out loud

Faces, faces, stretched with despair

Look at me, does anyone care?

Faces, faces, weathered with time

This face I wear, it's still mine

Faces, faces, the lines are deep

This is my face, the face I will keep

Measuring Time

How does one measure time?

By the years spent on this earth?

By what one has achieved while

Visiting this earth?

Maybe time is measured by success?

Maybe by one's failures in life?

By the disappointments along our

Journey?

Measuring of time is not what's

Important

Or how much time we spend on Earth

What is important is how we use this

Valuable time

Can your time spent here be accounted for?

If you can successfully account for your

Precious time

Then your living was not in vain

Reflecting

Am I a mirror reflecting my image

In reverse?

Not a true representation of my

Worth

Am I a mirror emulating what I see

Is that a true image of me?

Reflections

Looking in the mirror what do I see?

Me looking at me

Looking in the mirror

Everything is in reverse

Left is not left, right is a little worse

Looking in the mirror

Seeing what I see

Wondering where did I go

What happened to me?

Searching

What are we searching for?

A unifying thread to happiness

A major potion to longevity

Eternal satisfaction

Whatever it may be

Enjoy the time given

We are always

Searching, Searching, Searching

Sharing

Belonging, giving, and
togetherness

Responsibility

A part of what life has to offer

Wanting to be the half of a whole

Who AM I?

I am me

A reflection of God's creation

An image in a mirror

A mirror of our world

Looking at the emptiness, destruction

Caused by Man

Who AM I?

Part of a whole generations of me's

I's and Gimmies

A selfish self–destructed universe

Cursed by the cursers

MAN

Destroyer of the planet

Who AM I?

One of many stars trying to shine

Yesterday

Yesterday, today, forever

Never promised

Yesterday is today

Tomorrow is forever

Short but real

Enjoyed by few

Yesterday vanishes

Tomorrow anew

Faces change

Friendship strained

Feelings shattered

Insides battered

Yesterday is today

Tomorrow is forever

Hold on to forever

PART FOUR

Tough Love

Not in My Neighborhood

Destroyer and animal

Not in my neighborhood

You don't

You won't spread your infectious disease

Into our children, our future

With your sly lies, slick ways

Corroding the mind

You dare bring this in my

Neighborhood

We are a proud and strong family

Corruption will not enter our streets

Nor will it enter the minds of our

Young

Go away, stay away, or else

You will see the strength in unity

Not in my neighborhood you don't

Our Children

Children in Need

Of Direction, Hope, and Guidance

Society can't cope

Who are these children?

Children of a lost generation

Our future

Struggling in a corrupt world

Society put away your anger

Hide your Greed

These are our children

Children in Need

What Do You See?

We are producing a world

Of non–thinking humans

A growing society of

Functional Illiterates

Nurturing on a dumb cane

Sucking the life out of stupidity

Stumbling along side by side

With ignorance

Strangling the hell out of a wasted life

Destroying their being

Their purpose on this planet

Crawling around in darkness

Killing any and every

Digging an empty hole

Resembling their brain

PART FIVE

Eres Mi Todo

(You Are My Everything)

A Love Forever Can Never Be Lost

Turn back the hands of time

Relive those precious moments

Rejoice in the splendor of love

For today is not promised

Listen to your inner self

Believe in your feelings

For the gift of loving someone

Is a joy forever

Whispering

Whispering your name

Your sweet sounding name

Makes me feel alive inside

Whispering your name

So softly as I do

Holding on to every thought of you

While whispering your name

Loving You is a Pleasure

You touched my heart

You stole my soul

You made me woman

You made me whole

You opened up my world

Full of happiness and peace

You made me feel love again

To say the very least

You gave me you, so strong and tall

A treasure in itself to behold

So my dear, loving you is my pleasure

Amarte Es un Placer

Amarte es un Placer
(Loving You is a Pleasure)

Tú tocas mi corazón

Robaste mi alma

Me hiciste mujer

Me hiciste completa

Abriste mi mundo

Lo Llenaste de felicidad y paz

Me hiciste sentir amor de nuevo

Por decir menos

Me diste de ti, tan fuerte y alto

Un tesoro para contemplar

Asi que mi querido amarte es mi placer

Amarte es un placer

You Are My Everything

I can only tell you what I feel

A sensation of pure ecstasy

A divine calmness reaches my

inner soul

A rush of love supports my stance

Yes, my dear you are the strength

That supports my being

You are the light that

Illuminates my soul

You are the air I long to breathe

You are my every being

You are you

Eres Mi Todo
(You Are My Everything)

Solo puedo decirte lo que siento

Una sensacion de Extasis

Una calma divina alcanza mi alma

Una oleada de amor apoya mi postura

Sí, mi querido tú eres la fuerza

Que apoya mi ser

Tú eres la luz que ilumina mi alma

Eres el aire que deseo respirar

Eres todo para mi

Tú eres tú

With You

When I walk with you

I feel as if I'm walking with Kings

Making me feel like your Queen

Showering me with love

Touching me with your tenderness

While leading me to your kingdom

When I walk with you

I am safe, loved, and cherished

PART SIX

I Can Only Say
I'm Sorry

Darkness

A Human Being

Protector of this race

A race of beings fading away

Creating Disaster, Trouble, and Pain

Protecting What?

Their own Greed

Greed that will destroy the Race,

Universe, Planet

The light is slowly fading, fading

It's now dark

Disgruntled Faces

Disgruntled faces looking at me

Trying to do A, B, and C

Disgruntled faces so perplexed

Wondering what to do next

Disgruntled faces trying to understand

Doing the very best they can

Emptiness

A hollow feeling

Weightless

Without meaning

Or purpose

Nothing left inside

But Me

Freedom

You gave so much and received so little

I wonder if it's fair

You taught us love

You taught us hope

You taught us how to share

You strongly believed in equality

You fought for everyone's rights

But as I lay my head down at night

I still question your fight

Goodbye

Looking up you're standing there

Made me realize I didn't care

Searching my soul

Searching deep in my heart

Realizing that our separation

Was my start

There were bad times and hard times

That would have weakened any

Strong mind

I thank my God for making me strong

Seeing you again made it easy

To say so long

Groups

Where do we go from here?

I keep asking this question

Are we prepared to move on?

Or do we just mull and wither away?

I Can Only Say I'm Sorry

I Can Only Say I'm Sorry

For wasting so many years

Through this agonizing process

I was blinded by my tears

You take things for granted

Thoughts somewhat slanted

Dreams, Hopes, and Ideas disappear

I Can Only Say I'm Sorry

The years have quickly gone by

Maturity teaches many things

But the hurt still deep inside

Like A Rock

Like a rock I was there

Like a rock, strong no fear

Like a rock weathering the storm

Like a rock, fading away and worn

Like a rock, losing ground

Gone and no longer around

Somebody
(His Inner Thoughts)

She makes me feel like

Somebody

Her warmth, patience, tenderness

Surrounds her every movement

She makes me feel like

Somebody

Her smile, concern, and love

Easily displayed

She makes me feel like

Somebody

Arms open wide

When I'm tired and worried

She makes me feel like

Somebody

Never questioning me, always there

For me

She makes me feel like

Somebody

Praising me for who I am

Not rejecting me for what

I have not achieved

She makes me feel like

Somebody

Walking beside me, at times

Holding me up

She makes me feel like

Somebody

Always ready, willing, and able

To sustain my deepest pain

She makes me feel like

Somebody

She lifts up my lifeless body

She makes me feel like

Somebody

She is real

She is there

She is the other

WOMAN

The Other Cheek

Can't turn the other cheek

Still too bitter and not meek

Can't turn the other cheek

Can it be I'm too weak?

Can't turn the other cheek

Must be able to speak

Turn the other cheek

HOW?

Visions

Shadows of a memory

Past I can't see

Visions of objects

Somewhere around me

Stillness so quiet I can't hear

Emptiness so empty

Cannot bear

Waiting, Waiting, and Waiting

Sitting and waiting again you are late

What is really going on, don't I rate?

Once or twice I can excuse

Funny love, I get the feeling

I'm being used

PART SEVEN

My Faith Looks Up to Thee

Ain't So Bad

Ain't So Bad After All

I made my peace before you called

My soul is free from agony

My spirit is now with thee

Ain't So Bad After All

You had your reasons

I heard your call

Ain't So Bad After All

You're there to help if I fall

Ain't So Bad After All

Standing straight and tall

Christmas Gathering

As we sit by the Christmas tree

Family, friends, and me

We reflect on the passing year

Thanking HIM

We are all here

The year has been long and hard

Our faith is always in our GOD

Thankful for the many gifts on that day

The ooh's, ahh's, and words hard to say

This celebration blessed with faith and love

A gentle thanks for HIM above

Credence

When I cease to believe in the

Almighty

Then

I close my eyes

If

My faith is as strong as my

Will

Then

I have fulfilled my desires

Tears from Heaven

Tears from heaven touching your soul

Erase away the sins of our world

Cleanse our hearts with warm raindrops

Leaving a glow of peace

You Are My Tree

The tree of strength and stability

Growing to a considerable height

Your branches shading me from harm

You are my tree, strong, powerful, and fierce

You're not easily moved or shaken

Yet kindness sprouts from your limbs

You are a tree with deep passion and well-preserved

You are my tree of life

PART EIGHT

The End (For Now)

So What Do You Do With the Pictures?

So what do you do with the

Pictures?

You took all those many years

You carefully turn the pages,

Smile

And release the anger and fears

So what do you do with the

Pictures?

You hold tight to the memories

Be thankful for those precious

Years

Slowly close the book without

The bitter tears

73479484R00042

Made in the USA
Columbia, SC
12 July 2017